WELCOME TO
COLLEGE

YOUR CAREER STARTS NOW!

*A Practical Guide to
Academic and Professional Success*

VICTOR BROWN

Printed in the United States of America

First printing, 2019

Print ISBN: 978-1-54396-036-5
eBook ISBN: 978-1-54396-037-2

BookBaby Publishing
7905 North Crescent Boulevard
Pennsauken, NJ 08110
www.BookBaby.com

Dedication

To Denise and Our "Once and Future" College Students

Dave, Kristin, Steve, Valerie

...and little Jordan...

TABLE OF CONTENTS

INTRODUCTION

My friend called me one November day, asking for some help. It seems that her son, a college senior, was in a panic. He would be graduating in a few months, and did not yet have a job lined up - nor the slightest idea how to go about it.

Nevertheless, she knew I had taught for a number of years at the college level, was working on this book, and asked if I could speak with her son and perhaps give him some guidance as to how he might pursue his job search in an orderly fashion. Of course, I was happy to do so.

Although this may have seemed to my friend to be an unusual situation, sadly it is quite commonplace. Almost all of the students I taught were in their fourth year in college, and many were in a state of shock — how did the three previous years vanish so quickly, and what were they supposed to do about life after graduation - now looming in just a few months?

Although some of my students had spent time trying to sort this out, many really hadn't — and the question I encountered from them more than once was: "Do you know of any jobs out there"? Not jobs in a specific field for which they had been carefully preparing — just jobs, almost any jobs. Something to get them started.

It certainly doesn't have to be this way, and shouldn't.

This book is intended to assist you during two different life transitions. The first is to help you, as a new college student, think clearly about how to select a major and work toward a long term career direction, and how to best prepare for it in terms of curriculum, internships and possibly a semester abroad. All of these decisions build on one another, and it is important to start the process as soon as possible.

You have some time, of course, and your plans may well change along the way. But a foundation carefully laid will allow you to adjust as you go, in the least disruptive manner. Importantly, you want to avoid realizing that you took too many of the "wrong" courses, and did not make optimum use of your internships and possible study abroad opportunities.

You also want to begin to lay the groundwork for your post-graduate career. As you grow though your college years, and sharpen your focus on required and elective courses, you will need to begin thinking seriously about how this preparation will help you to move into a career that will match your interests and college experience, and continue to build upon this excellent foundation.

Secondly, this book may assist you during your transition into full time employment, as it applies many of the same principles to the different - but in many ways similar - demands of the workplace.

Much of the advice I offer also addresses the very personal side of your preparation. We will talk at length about how the development of highly effective personal behaviors can help you to establish yourself as a serious, professional person — in college and in the workplace.

I learned much of this through my own trial and error, but also by observing the personal traits exhibited by successful students and professional colleagues.

I majored in chemistry at a small liberal arts college and earned an MBA at a major university while pursuing a long, satisfying career with a large, diversified manufacturer of chemicals and machinery.

After retirement, I embarked on a second career on the faculty and staff of a well-regarded liberal arts college. It was there that I taught courses in management, marketing and international business. The content of these courses reflected the knowledge I had acquired during my career.

The corporate years gave me insight into what kinds of people made progress, earned promotions, and in general were able to enjoy vibrant careers.

Teaching, on the other hand, gave me fresh insight into how students thought (or in some cases did not think) about life after college, and what behaviors they were exhibiting in the classroom that would later help or hinder their own career development.

Based on all of this, then, I have developed a perspective on how I think students can make the greatest use of their college education, and how they can use those short four years as a launching pad for a successful career.

Part of college and career success depends upon what you learn from your courses and related academic activity. Part depends upon the skill set you develop. A surprisingly large measure depends on your personal style — and how you present yourself to others.

Although addressed primarily to students entering and graduating from college, this book can be informative reading for many others who may benefit from its guidance and recommendations:

High school teachers and college guidance counselors.

College faculty and career services advisors.

College administrators, who are responsible for ensuring that the appropriate kinds of academic and career guidance support are in place and readily available to the students.

Parents of students - who are concerned about making the most of the expensive college investment, and are rightly interested in seeing you move into a rewarding career.

Executives, managers and human resource personnel in professional organizations, who are seeking to build workplace competencies.

I welcome this opportunity to share my experiences and insights, as you are critically important. You represent our next generation of leaders, about to move from campus to career, and on to positions of leadership in business and society.

It all starts with the four years in college, which will be over almost in an instant. You are now largely on your own, even though you have the support of faculty advisors, parents, and others. You will need to select your electives, internships and other activities to prepare you for a long and prosperous career. You will also need to develop a personal and professional style that sets you apart from your peers, and prepares you for success on campus and in the years ahead.

PART ONE
The College Years

CHAPTER 1

Choice of college is not as important as what you do with it

You may have chosen to attend a large state university, a small liberal arts college, or to start with (and maybe finish with) a community college. In my view, any of those choices are absolutely fine. In higher education one size does not fit all, and the choice of a school is a highly individualized decision, one in which many factors come into play.

I attended a small college; some of the colleagues I worked with over the years had graduated from such notable schools as Harvard, Penn and Yale — yet, we all seemed to experience similar career paths.

No matter what college you attend, you will have good and poor instructors, good and poor course content, good and poor social experiences. In my opinion, your future success will depend upon you - not upon your choice of college or university.

The Ivy League colleges may tell you that it's all about connections, and tapping into their close-knit network of alumni. To some extent, all colleges have alumni who can help in the initial stages of your career. What matters most is not where you ultimately choose to work after graduation, but how you perform once you get there. My sincere hope is that you won't need too much in the way of alumni support anyway, as you will be making your own excellent impressions on the employers who will be intensely interested in you.

Your college years offer the opportunity to learn to manage on your own, away from the "parental units". It's a time to develop your own personal and professional style — how to manage your time, meet your obligations and get the most out of the exposure you will now have to academic information, professors, campus speakers and events.

It's also the time to develop your own professional persona — how you dress, how you speak, how you stay ahead of the curve in all of your courses, and how you develop and articulate positions on complex issues. Parental influence wanes during these years. Now is the time for you to identify and draw upon other sources of positive influence.

Many will tell you that college provides a chance to explore. They say not to worry too much about taking courses that are directly tied to your future work environment, but to instead sample all of the "academic delights" that a college can offer. This is the "learn to think, your employer will train you later in what they need" school of thought.

Others will say that college is primarily a time to begin to delve deeply into one field of study, to prepare for your career, and that there is no substitute for getting a job and career that pays well.

Both approaches are correct, in my view. The trick is to do both in a way that makes sense for you, and we will discuss this when we talk about how to use your elective courses.

To emphasize the importance of all of this, I will share with you an unfortunate college statistic. Approximately 40% of enrolled students never get a degree, even in six years. Perhaps they drop out early (many do, especially after the first year). But some of these students are simply unfocused, switch majors a number of times, and finally run out of gas on the college experience — short of achieving their degree.

You don't want to be counted in that statistic, and the best way to achieve an on-time degree is to be focused, diligent and striving to coordinate your college experience with your career plan.

CHAPTER 2

How do I choose a major?

E veryone asks you the same question — "What do you plan to major in"? As you enter college, many of you really aren't too sure, and have selected a school that offers a fairly wide selection of possible majors. Your plan is to get started in college, and to decide this "major" thing along the way.

Some students, of course, have made the decision well in advance. One of my sons had planned while in high school to major in meteorology, so he went to Penn State - which by all accounts has one of the world's leading programs in that discipline.

Most students fall somewhere in between these two poles. You have a general idea of what you would like to study, but have not quite focused it to the point of making a decision about a major. This is fine, but college is expensive and you want to graduate in as few years as possible, so this is a decision you will need to deal with seriously, and without too much delay.

I would encourage every incoming college student to think hard about what they are "good" at, academically speaking. For some, science and math are the strong suits, and for them a major in math, chemistry, physics or biology may be the best route (I was a chemistry major). For others, the written word is more appealing, which leads to majors in such areas as English and history. For still others, aptitude in the creative arts leads in yet another direction, towards music, voice, art and the like.

Remember that the selection of a major course of study is your choice. By all means, draw upon the good advice of others, but in the final analysis make it your decision. You know yourself better than anyone else does.

So, try to discern a general discipline of study that makes sense for you, based on answering the simple questions "What do I do well, and what do I enjoy?" You already know the answers, if you think about it a bit. Remember to always play to your strengths. There is no sense trying to build a college or work career around subject matter that you find too difficult or frustrating. That will just work against your growth goals.

On the other hand, thoroughly enjoying what you do will generate the verve and enthusiasm that shines through to others, and your chances of academic and career success will be greatly increased.

Later in this book, we will spend time talking more specifically about career choices. Although the choice of major and the choice of career are certainly closely related, they are not quite the same thing.

For example, a biology major may wish to go on to graduate school, gain a PhD in biology, and work in a research setting. A fellow biology major may want to pursue a career in sales and marketing with a pharmaceutical company. Both will build their careers on the biology degree foundation, but use it to go into two different directions. This is where personal preference comes into play. For example, many researchers are not comfortable in a sales setting, while many sales people are simply not very good at laboratory work - myself included, which is why I went into chemical sales after college!

The point that I would like to make here is that any college degree can offer a number of career avenues. Don't think that by majoring in chemistry you need to go on to grad school for a doctorate and spend your career in a research lab, as useful as that is to society. You may choose to go on to grad school for an MBA, and pursue a career in the commercial functions of a company involved with petrochemicals — also a rewarding and useful career.

I'll share with you an example of what can happen if these things are not considered in a timely fashion.

Every semester, I taught a class in international business, and almost all of my students were seniors. Since I had spent three decades in the chemical industry, a number of the case studies we discussed in class were based on actual cases I had encountered during my career. One of the students in the course was a chemistry major, in his final semester at the college. He told me that, until taking my course, he had no idea that there was any option open to a chemistry major other than a career in research. Although he had planned to pursue the research route, he decided to change direction and pursue a career in the commercial end of that business.

The frustrating part was that, had he realized all of this sooner, he could have used his elective courses to support his new direction — courses such business law, economics, marketing and management. I believe this student was not well served by his faculty advisor, which is why you need to take the lead in setting your own program of studies.

Most colleges give you until the end of your sophomore year to select a major. My preference is for students to make this selection by the end of their first year. With the high price of college, as well as for the reasons we have just discussed, try to make the selection of a major your goal for the end of your first year in school.

So how exactly do you go about thinking through this selection of a major? Based on my experience, I would offer the following suggestions.

Save those free electives until after your first, and possibly second, year.

At the college where I taught, it generally took 32 courses to graduate. Somewhere between 10-12 of these were courses specific to the department in which you majored. Another 10-12 were courses selected to meet the college liberal arts "core requirements", which are designed to give all students a well-rounded education. Finally, there were about 10 courses that were "free electives" and could be selected from almost any course taught on campus.

The interesting thing to note is that those 10-12 courses required as part of the "core" can actually be taken from a list that is many times longer — several science courses will meet the science core requirement, several history courses will meet the core requirement in that area, etc. Carefully review your college's catalog, and you will be surprised at the degree of flexibility that you actually have in selecting courses.

In your first year, take as many courses as you can that you will actually need to meet graduation requirements — you will have many to choose from, and you can thereby save those previous "free electives" for your final two years — as my chemistry major student wishes he had done!

Many colleges will encourage students to "sample the academic delights" during the first two years, and then settle into the major field of study. In my opinion, there are plenty of delights to be sampled as part of the required first year and core courses.

Some say that college is an opportunity to learn to think and be creative; others say it is a place to prepare for a career. I think, by being a judicious selector of courses, it can be both!

Double major? Major and minor?

My recommendation is to focus on one major, and complement it with the electives that will help you the most. Majoring in chemistry, with a minor in art, might sound nice and be a lot of fun but it won't cut much mustard with employers operating in the chemical industry. Conversely, if applying for a position at an art museum, the hiring manager will wonder why you didn't decide to major in art.

Better for a business major, say, to complement the core business courses (accounting, finance, marketing, etc.) with electives that fit well in a multinational business environment —international trade, global economic systems, antitrust law, etc. Developing such a well-thought out curriculum is a big plus.

Our art major, on the other hand, may want to supplement the art curriculum with selected courses in marketing, management, organizational behavior, advertising, etc. — after all, everything is a business (as any museum or artistic director will tell you).

A double major simply crowds out too many free electives, in my opinion. A minor course of study is just that - relatively minor, not that many courses, and really quite secondary to your primary career goals. Keep the free electives truly free and highly useful — pick one major, and design your own set of complementary "academic delights"!

Don't dread the foreign language requirement - embrace it!

I know, I know. Many students absolutely hate the idea that they need to take a foreign language in college, and even their very college selection decision can depend on how many semesters of foreign language study are required. They moan and groan, and do their best to "test out" of at least one semester of this nonsense.

But they are missing a great opportunity by doing so. Facility in a foreign language is a real asset in almost any endeavor in our globalized society. Yes, English is the universal language in aviation and certainly the common language of upper management in most organizations, but it is far from a universal language. The ability to speak and understand a major language (such as French, German, Mandarin, and Spanish) can prove to be a valuable skill.

In high school, I was "forced" to take four years of German, and the college I attended required two years of a language, so I continued with German. By that time, I was developing a fair degree of proficiency and decided to take a final two years of German that focused heavily on speaking and listening comprehension.

As it happens, much of the global chemical industry is based in Germany, and I traveled there frequently to meet with customers, suppliers and partners. My ability to converse in German made a real impression on them — and gave me an edge over many of my competitors, who had never bothered to learn the language.

Language is one of those skills that can come into play in unexpected ways. My advice is to pick one, and master it. It is almost certain to prove useful, in ways you may not even anticipate.

Discuss your curriculum game plan with your faculty advisor.

Most likely, your first faculty advisor will be selected for you almost at random. The advisor will help you walk through the first semester course registration process at orientation, and meet with you one or twice during the first year to see how you are doing.

This would be the time to let your advisor know your game plan — to take courses in the first two years (and certainly the first year) that will fulfill a graduation requirement in some way, such as the core curriculum and the special courses that are often required of first year students.

Once you do select a major, your assigned faculty advisor will be a member of that department, if not already the case. Continue to discuss your career aspirations with your advisor on a regular basis, and get as much guidance as you can.

Bear in mind that you can avail yourself of many faculty advisors, not just the "official" advisor whose primary concern may well be to ensure that you earn enough credits for graduation.

There are many faculty members on campus who are willing to speak with you, share their experiences and judgment, and in general become part of your curriculum major and career decision making. You will meet some of these faculty members in class. Others you will have heard about from class-mates. Don't be shy — feel free to approach any of them for advice.

Maybe this is also the time to talk about "adjunct faculty". These men and women are not full-time members of the faculty, and are neither tenured nor tenure-track. Some of them do want to be tenured, and are teaching as adjuncts until an opportunity might open up for them.

But many are involved in careers of their own, and teach a course or two in college for the love of it. Believe me, it's certainly not for the money! Adjunct faculty members are notoriously poorly paid, so these faculty with full-time careers are on campus because they want to share their knowledge of the sub-ject, and help you in any way possible. They represent an excellent source of advice and guidance for you.

Engage other partners in your decision making process.

I worked closely with career guidance staff at the college, and I know one of their greatest frustrations was that students would wait until much too late to begin using their services. You may not be ready to apply for your first full-time job until your senior year, but that doesn't mean you should wait that long to begin to speak with them about your choice of a major, and what career options may be available to you.

Just as with your faculty advisor, don't hesitate to engage a member of the career service staff as your career advisor, and work with this person from the outset, discussing not only your choice of major and longer-term career options, but also any intermediate internship opportunities that may support you in achieving that goal.

CHAPTER 3

Creating your image as a serious student

Personal behavior is critically important in the workplace, as it can differentiate you from others in terms of how well you present yourself, how effectively you engage with business partners, and how well you are considered by management for promotions and increased levels of responsibility in the organization.

Just as in college, you will be surrounded by people who are very bright and talented. But not all of them will exhibit the same level of highly developed positive personal characteristics. It is important to understand that many of the behavioral patterns that you learn in college will carry directly over into the workplace, so in this book we will talk about them in both contexts. It's that important.

Don't underestimate how important your personal image can be in college. The one you want to develop and project is one that is professional and serious.

Attention to the task at hand is the first priority. Focusing on doing each task as well as you possibly can will help you to develop the traits that will allow you to accomplish your longer-term objectives. So let's talk about some specific behaviors that you should develop right away.

Class preparation.

Always come to class prepared to discuss the readings and assignments. Make notes on your key questions and observations, in advance of class discussion. This will not just demonstrate that you have mastered the material, but it indicates to your professor and fellow students that you want to learn as much as possible from the material in question.

During class, take meaningful (not necessarily copious) notes. A good instructor will provide many of the lecture materials separately and during class will just focus on the key points for discussion. Therefore, jot down the major points and listen intently for the discussion and detail behind those points. Class time should not be a memorization challenge, and usually is not.

Don't procrastinate.

When a case study or similar paper is assigned for delivery in several weeks, get started right away. Begin to research the topic and construct an outline of your paper. This will then give you time to reflect on your paper's development, improve the content and flow, and ask others to offer their opinions and advice on what you have written.

I always encouraged my students to meet with me once they had a fairly well developed outline, and we would then discuss the direction and flow of the paper. This invariably gave the students a very good idea of what the paper should look like, and the finished product was almost always quite good.

Unfortunately, however, many students did not avail themselves of this opportunity, primarily because they procrastinated and did not begin to work seriously on the document until almost the last minute. As a result, those papers were almost always more poorly written — and graded accordingly.

If your professor does not offer you an opportunity to discuss your paper in its interim state, feel free to ask. I can't imagine a professor who would not be willing to offer this assistance.

Develop a crisp, clean writing style.

One of the major complaints that employers have about new graduates is the quality of their writing. Attention to this from your first semester will give you a running start in developing the type of writing style that will allow you to excel, both in your coursework as well as in the workplace.

Most good papers will capture the essence of the issue (and your conclusion) in one or two initial paragraphs that will comprise your "executive summary". You will find that it is surprisingly difficult to condense the contents of your paper to a few sentences. But condense it you must, so your instructor (and, later, your future boss) will know that you possess critical thinking skills and can summarize complex issues succinctly.

Organization of the paper is extremely important. Judicious use of headings and sub-headings, as well as bullet points on occasion, will provide an excellent road map for the reader. This "form" is just as important as your paper's "substance".

Be aggressive in separating paragraphs. I cannot tell you how often I encountered paragraphs written by students that rambled on for an entire page, and on occasion over several pages. The guidance that I urge you to follow is "new thought = new paragraph".

Always conclude your paper with a good summary of the issue at hand, why it is important, and why you reached the conclusion you did. If there is further research recommended, then include that as well with a summary of the "next steps" that you would recommend.

Watch the details. Watch them!

As a writer, I have poured over my manuscripts, looking for any and all possible misspellings, typos and violations of good grammar and word selection. Then I am shocked, once the work is in print, to see one or two that I somehow missed.

Be diligent. If your paper exhibits poor attention to these details, the reader will assume that your content is similarly slipshod, and may not take the time to read it.

The most popular word processors have built-in spelling and grammar checks, so use them as a first pass. Then review the document again and again for mistakes that even these software programs do not always identify.

Finally, use professional words. For example, a purchasing agent doesn't write in a memo that he will "stick with" a supplier, but he writes that he will "remain with" a supplier. Always think about how you can use more polished, more professional choices of words and phrases.

Seize every opportunity to present to the class.

Often, the instructor will want you to present your paper's findings to the class as a whole. Although many students are intimidated by this, it represents a great opportunity to learn how to make professional presentations - which you will be called upon to do many times over the course of your career.

Microsoft's "PowerPoint" and Apple's "Keynote" are excellent software packages to use for your presentation, so select the one that is most compatible with your laptop.

The important thing is to use the slides as a guide for the audience - and not for a lot of detail. As you discuss your paper, you may well want to have several points on the slides that highlight your sources, the key arguments pro and con, and your conclusions.

But make these simple points only, advancing through the slides as you go. It will help the audience to follow your explanation, without getting bogged down in too much information on the slide. You want your audience listening to you, not reading detailed slides as you speak.

Read, read.....then read some more.

Digital content is everywhere, and it seems at times that we are drowning in television, radio and social media information. We won't be able to change this easily, but we can do the next best thing as we develop our professional image.

Content that is read is almost always more impactful than listening to spoken arguments and general media hype. I always encouraged my students to not only read what was assigned, but to go beyond that and read to develop themselves as informed, serious students.

The Wall Street Journal and The New York Times are generally recommended. They have different perspectives on events but, by reading each of them, students can begin to understand the best arguments on both sides of any issue, and form their own well-developed conclusions. There are many other journals, of course, that are extremely informative, and your library will have them on hand.

Often, you will read book reviews or receive recommendations from others about books that are interesting to you. Make a note of these titles and make an effort to read as many of these books as possible. Keep a list of the books, and then check them off as you finish them. When a potential employer asks you what books you have read recently, refer to the list. It's a very effective and impressive way of answering the question.

CHAPTER 4

Let's get personal

The things we have discussed thus far are focused on your preparation, participation and study habits, and they are all very important.

Just as important, however, is the way in which you "carry" yourself. It's now time for you to start adopting a personal style that will prepare you for success on campus and in the workplace.

After graduation, you will likely find yourself in an organization surrounded by very bright, capable people. But trust me — not all of them will have spent their college years learning how to relate to others in an appropriate professional manner. By developing and exhibiting a high level of what I like to call "personal deportment", you will make strong, positive and lasting impressions on others.

Correct personal behaviors come into play in two ways. The first is the positive impression you make on your colleagues and management. Secondly, other people with whom you interface - customers, suppliers, and other stakeholders - will appreciate how professionally you represent your own organization, and this will often filter back to your management and thus will serve to place you in a positive light.

So let's talk a bit about the personal behaviors that my best students never failed to exhibit. When we get to a later chapter in this book, we will revisit some of these behaviors in the context of the workplace environment.

Be on time.

Look all around you. Everywhere you see "internet time" displayed - absolutely correct time on watches, laptops, iPads, computers, televisions, and digital devices of all types. Unlike the old days, every clock is now exactly in sync, and this is how the world operates, in a closely choreographed dance of meetings, emails, texts and phone calls.

There's good reason for this. Society today is highly collaborative. The agricultural economy has given way to a digitally enabled manufacturing and service economy. People work together on projects as never before, and this work is spread effectively among individuals who can be located almost anywhere in the world.

Of course, this interconnectedness depends on people being available for each other when they are required to be. You can imagine the embarrassment if a news anchor throws a story to a journalist in Tel Aviv - and he's running ten minutes late!

The same applies on campus. Classes are tightly scheduled, and they generally only run 50 minutes or so, which is why it is important for students and instructors alike to be there on time, ready to go. Those 50 minutes will be gone in a blink of an eye, and there's much material to cover.

As we will discuss later, some executives have a habit of being the last person to show up for a meeting. They think their time is more important than anyone else's, so they will not arrive until all others are present.

Unfortunately, some faculty will adopt the same approach, and always walk in five minutes after class is scheduled to start. In both cases, it shows a lack of respect for employees and students, and reflects very poorly on the person who is late.

In my courses, 20% of a student's grade was based on "class engagement" — and part of that was being on time. I promised my students that I would always be on time, and I expected them to do the same. In fact, I was always in class 5-10 minutes early, getting the AV equipment set up and ensuring that we were ready to go.

So my advice is to develop the habit of being on time - for class, for meetings, for conferences with faculty members, and for scheduled commitments you will have later in the workplace. Those around you may not fully appreciate your promptness, but they will surely notice any tardiness.

Pay attention.

It was always so obvious. As in all colleges, students use their laptops and iPads to take notes and download slides from the instructor's file. All well and good. But of course there is always the temptation to use the devices to check emails and texts, catch up on Facebook feeds, and the like. As I walked around the room during class discussion, I could spot the "Facebook gaze" in a second, and would always direct a question in that student's direction. Shocked into sudden attention, the student would ask me to repeat the question. I never did, though, and the student suffered the obvious embarrassment of being caught napping, and getting dinged on the "class engagement" thing!

Please don't make that mistake, in class or anywhere else. There's plenty of time later for Facebook. Your instructors and fellow students deserve your attention, and you deserve theirs. So sit up straight, exhibit a personal energy level as you engage in "active listening" and draw as much information as you can from every encounter. It's a habit that you will be glad you developed, because the consequences for any non-attention will be much greater, later on.

Dress appropriately.

Note that I did not say coat and tie, tailored suit, or anything of the like. After all, you are in college, and a certain degree of causal dress is the order of most days.

There will be occasions where you will want to don that suit, such as when you present your final course paper to the class, or the results of your research to a group of faculty members. Looking sharp and professional in those circumstances will be a real plus, since most of your campus time will be spent in more casual attire.

Most of all, dress for what *might* happen today, not what you *think* will happen. You may be called into a Dean's office for some reason, or asked to meet spur of the moment with visiting alumni donors or prospective students. In smaller colleges, you may even end up spending a few minutes with the college president. So, you will want to be sure you look good, look serious, and look respectful. Once again, these are good habits to form — and later on, you will be glad you did.

Watch your language — please!

This might be a good time to mention the options for addressing your instructors on campus. Some of them will hold doctorate degrees in their fields, and may wish to be addressed as "Doctor". Others may or may not hold doctorates, and prefer "Professor". Still others, especially adjuncts, may prefer "Mr." or "Ms.". A very, very few (mistaken, in my opinion) will ask you to address them by their first names, but never do so unless invited. All in all, "Professor" is fine for use with all faculty.

In terms of language in the classroom, I think you know what I am about to suggest. There are words (and you know what they are) that simply have no place in a college or professional setting. Never use them, as it shows a lack of respect for your colleagues, and suggests that you have personal standards that are less than those acceptable in professional settings.

Other colloquial terms can be upgraded, and you should get used to doing so. For example, a "guy" can be referred to as a man, just as the college age "girl" should be referred to as a woman. That sort of thing.

Always use a moderate tone of voice. No shouting, no speaking so low that others strain to hear you, no "hard edge" — but just a conversational, objective, pleasant voice. It all counts.

Make sure your "body language" matches your professional style. Sit up straight, no slouching. Lean forward slightly to show you are focused and attentive. Practice the art of "active listening" while doing your best to block out other distractions and focus on what is being shared by your instructors and classmates.

Let me share one other little secret in this regard. I could always identify, from the first minute of the first class each semester, the good students. They were the ones who entered the classroom and sat up front. They were always, always the most serious students. Those who headed for the back row? Not so much, and this pattern persisted without fail for all of my thirteen years teaching in the college classroom.

CHAPTER 5

Choosing a career path

O nce you have selected a major field of study, hopefully by the end of your first year in college, you can begin to think about the various ways in which you can put that curriculum to work after graduation. As you sharpen your thinking on this, you can begin to select course electives that will support your career objective.

To use our earlier example, a biology major who decides to enter into pharmaceutical research might start taking a number of scientific electives that point toward a graduate science degree, while the biology major heading into commercial aspects of the pharmaceutical industry may start taking elective courses in marketing and finance.

Working with students over the years, I have found that a systematic approach to considering career options works best. As with many difficult decisions, it is best to start at the most general level, and then work down to consider more specific alternatives.

Start with a list of the largest organizations, ranked in several ways — by sales revenue, number of employees, market capitalization, markets served, etc. These can be for-profit corporations like Microsoft and Ford, or they can be non-profit organizations like the Red Cross, government agencies, educational institutions, etc.

These lists are readily available in your college library and career services office, and the staff in those departments can assist you. For example, the "Fortune 500" is a list of the largest corporations by sales revenue, and similar lists are available through publications such as BusinessWeek, The Wall Street Journal and local business papers.

The next step is to carefully read through these lists with a pen and paper — lots of paper, actually. You are not yet looking at the companies themselves, but you are now focused on the types of industries or markets in which they operate. Write down every industry that appeals to you in any way, is in some way related to your major course of studies, and one in which you think you would be comfortable spending your career.

You will find that your list is quite long, and it might surprise you a bit. You may find the food industry to be interesting, but the brewing industry unattractive. You may be intrigued by high technology industries, but turned off by defense contractors. But, for starters, be sure to include any that have even the least bit of appeal.

Wait a few days, and then review your list with fresh eyes. Cross out the entries that, upon further reflection, do not belong on your list. You will feel your focus sharpening already.

Now you will want to rank those industries in rough order of preference, and begin to take a closer look at each one of them. Start by looking at the leading organizations in each area. It might be Apple in software and Ford in automotive, for example. Read about them, see what markets they serve, the products or services they provide, and how the information on their web sites appeals to you.

Begin now to cross-link your preferred industries with the largest organizations in each. The larger organizations, of course, have the most jobs to fill in any give year, and offer the most opportunities for career advancement.

With this refined, cross-referenced list in hand, look again at the organizations' web sites. Focus on their career sections and the types of positions are they advertising. These will include functions such as sales, marketing, manufacturing, accounting, finance, human resources, research and business development. As you review these job functions, begin to also make a list of the ones that interest you.

There is no doubt that this is a time-consuming process, and needs to be done over the course of several months. But it will challenge you and get you to focus more clearly on what you want to do after graduation, while that commencement ceremony draws ever closer.

Planning your internships and work-study programs.

Just as you want to orient your required and elective courses towards your now-developing career plan, you will want to do the same with your internship opportunities, some of which are available during the school year, and others during the summer breaks.

Your career services office is "internship central" and they list all sorts of opportunities provided by local companies, organizations in which alumni work, etc. Sit down with the career service staff member assigned to you, review your academic plan and career thoughts as they now exist, and ask the counselor to help you decide which internship opportunities might fit best with your emerging plan.

Most internships will come to you this way, but not all. I am reminded of a student I had in one of my classes. He was absolutely one of the brightest and most resourceful students I had the pleasure to teach. He sat in the front row (!), asked great questions and took the opportunity to speak with my various guest speakers after class.

One such speaker was a friend who worked for many years as Assistant General Counsel for his company, and he came to campus once each semester to speak to the students about antitrust law. It turns out that my student was planning to go to law school and he asked the guest speaker if his company ever hired summer interns to work in the law department. The visiting attorney replied that they had not, but asked the student for his resume. You guessed it — the student was hired to work full time during the summer between his third and fourth academic years, and was further engaged part-time during his senior year. The company loved him, gave a great recommendation for his law school applications, and the student went on for his law degree.

Good internship opportunities can come from almost anywhere. You just need to be on the lookout and always thinking about how your interaction with a faculty member, guest speaker, or visiting alum can work in your favor.

Do you plan to study abroad?

If so, this can be another important way in which you can build your resume and your knowledge of organizations that fit into your career plans.

I'm not sure how many college students spend a semester or a year abroad, but at most colleges I think it is as many as a third of the students, and almost always during the third year of study. Students select partner universities in Europe, Latin America and Asia, and the experiences are well planned and well supported.

When they returned, I always asked the students how well they liked the semester abroad. Usually I received replies that said it was a great experience, that they saw much of the local area and that their family members came over to join them for some vacation time. They said they appreciated the opportunity to learn about the art and the architecture, and to immerse themselves in the local culture.

If you return with these types of answers, and if you have previously taken the time and effort to develop a career plan along the lines that we have been discussing, you might not have made the most of this opportunity.

My suggestion would be to examine in advance the global operations of the organizations you are considering joining. See what facilities they may have around the world, and what geographic matches might exist between their operations and the places that you are considering for study abroad.

With this understanding, contact these organizations (we will talk soon about who specifically to approach). Explain to them your field of study, why you view them as possible career opportunities, and indicate that you would like to gain a deeper understanding of their operations.

Let them know that when you are in Rome, or London, or wherever you plan to study, you would welcome the opportunity to visit and possibly (depending on applicable regulations) work part time in one of their global offices. If this were to work out, it will give you a feel for their own local culture, their markets and products/services. It could also provide an eventual entree into the organization on a basis that most other applicants will not be able to match.

Your college, if they offer study abroad, has expert staff that will assist you in this effort; by all means, take advantage of what they and the career services department may have to offer.

CHAPTER 6

Launching your career

T hat certainly didn't take long! You have been very busy, adjusting to college, working hard in your courses, expanding your horizons, selecting a major and developing a good idea of what you want to do after you graduate. If you planned your time well, you probably even managed to fit in a party or two along the way!

Now here you are, in your final year of college, ready to go. No wandering the halls asking if anyone "knows of any jobs out there". Not for you, as you have done the good work necessary to position yourself for the critical next step — the job interview.

At the outset, let me say that employers need good employees just as much as you need a job. The lifeblood of any organization is its intellectual and human capital, and the well-educated and well-prepared graduate is a target for the organization's recruiting efforts. So don't be shy, or unsure of yourself. You have prepared well, and it is now about to show.

This may be the time to mention that you should establish a professional media presence. It costs almost nothing to purchase a domain name, which you can use to build your own personal web site.

Also be sure to establish a profile on LinkedIn, which is the professional equivalent of Facebook. While we're at it, look at your Facebook profile and delete anything that reminds you of the relatively immature person you used to be! Employers will do online searches, and you want only the best information out there.

Although each organization has its own method of evaluating applications, all of them will request a copy of your resume. Some, but not all, will ask for a cover letter as well. In my opinion, the cover letter is actually the more important of these two documents, and particularly so if you have followed the guidance set forth in this book.

Your career service staff will assist you in putting together your resume in a professional manner, and you should create the initial version of your resume during the first year of college. Update it at regular intervals as you select a major, engage in outside internships, and acquire other related experiences.

The fact is that most resumes look pretty much alike. They indicate the experiences - academic and otherwise - that you have *had*. It's the cover letter that tells the prospective employer where you want to *go*, and why.

It is in the cover letter that you indicate why you have selected this industry for a career, why you have selected this particular organization as a place to launch that career, and how you have carefully chosen academic courses, specific internships and possibly engaged in a particular study abroad program — all to support your career objective.

The important thing to stress in the cover letter is that you are not seeking just the job they happen to be advertising right now. Rather, you are seeking a career in an organization where you can grow into successive levels of responsibility, learn new skills with each position, and then bring those accumulated skills to your next assignment. If done properly, this sequence of positions will result in a "win-win" for you and the organization.

As a graduating student articulating all of this in a cover letter, you will most assuredly set yourself apart from your competition, and it will be well nigh impossible for a hiring manager not to be impressed with this degree of fore-sight, planning and thought.

But you need to get this wonderful cover letter to the right person! By all means, send your resume and cover letter to the company through the website that most of them have set up to handle applications. But don't stop there, since yours will be one of perhaps thousands of applications flooding into the company, and there is always a chance that the person doing the screening will not pick up on your preparation and planning.

Try to identify an additional person (or two) inside the organization to whom you can send your resume and cover letter, and ask them to forward it along to colleagues who may be looking for someone with your skills and career goals. It will be hard for this person not to read your cover letter in its entirety, and sending it along to HR with an endorsement may encourage the hiring manager to give you a good deal of consideration.

How do you identify such contacts in the organization? The best way is by personal referral from a professor, campus guest speaker, friend of the family, a neighbor, or whoever may have any contact inside the target organization. It doesn't have to be the hiring manager, just someone who can forward your thoughtful material to the right person.

If all else fails, select a person from the organization's website who looks like a possible initial contact, has an email address listed on the site, and then email that person. Once again, you should state that you know your addressee is not the hiring manager, but you are asking for this addressee to kindly forward your material to the right people inside the organization for consideration.

A friend of mine uses this technique frequently, especially when he wants to bring product or service issues to the attention of a company's upper manage-ment. Often, a company's investor relations personnel will have their email addresses listed on the company web site, and my friend finds that they are usually happy to route his emails to the proper person. How much more willing will they be to send along a cover letter and resume from a bright and impressive applicant!

Successful interviewing.

There are many good books that will help prepare you for a successful job interview. For our purposes here, though, let me discuss a number of things that you should think about as you prepare for that discussion. It may initially be a phone interview, but a successful phone interview often results in a personal follow-up meeting.

Confirm with your contact the specific timing and location of the appointment - and don't be late! Ideally, arrive a half hour prior to the appointed time, to allow for any problems with traffic or other delays.

For a telephone interview, dial in a minute or two ahead of time. You don't want to be the last person to enter the call.

Research the organization at length, and prepare to show as much familiarity as possible with their organization, products, services, competition, challenges, public relations presence, etc.

Ask them what their primary strategic goals are, what are the competing organizations or technologies with which they are most concerned, and how do they go about building and maintaining a quality organization that can meet these challenges.

Project enthusiasm. Sit up straight, listen intently, make a note or two if there are topics mentioned on which you would like to follow up. Also, don't be shy about having a list of topics that you gleaned from your preparation, things you would like to ask about in some depth. All of this shows a high level of interest and energy on your part.

Dress the part. The organization may have a formal dress code, or a more relaxed business casual environment. It doesn't matter, and don't ask ahead of time. Wear a nice suit and look your professional best.

Be sure to stress that you are seeking a career, not just a job. Indicate to the interviewers that you would like to learn and contribute as much as you can, hopefully in roles of increasing exposure and opportunity over time.

Ask them what they look for in an employee, and respond as honestly as you can as to how well you think you can meet those requirements. My guess is that, by this time, you will already be demonstrating the traits they desire.

Express willingness and a desire to return to meet others in the organization, if that is advisable.

At the conclusion, always ask about next steps. Each organization will have its own process for follow up discussions and final candidate selection. There is nothing wrong in asking about the path forward.

As soon as possible after the interviews, send an email follow up to each person with whom you met, thanking them for their time, asking if there is any other information that you can provide, and letting them know that you look forward to your next conversation.

In addition, send a personal handwritten note to the person who was your primary contact during the discussions. It does not have to be long, just a personal note of thanks for the opportunity to meet with them and discuss the position. Have that note in the mail the next morning!

PART TWO
The Early Career Years... and Beyond

Congratulations on receiving your degree, and welcome now to the "world of work"! You are likely to spend the next several decades earning a living, further developing your skills, and making positive contributions to society.

You are now well prepared for this phase of your life, and I think you will find it to be a marvelous and energizing time, if my own experience is any guide.

This second part of our book will offer my suggestions on how to establish yourself in the early years of your career, but it also includes advice relative to things that you may not encounter for several years, after you have grown and expanded your responsibilities. Nevertheless, I offer all of them here in the hope that you will keep this book as a reference, and take the time to re-read it periodically.

In the course of my business career, it was my privilege to deal in the business world with a broad spectrum of competent and professional individuals. These include fellow employees as well as others whom we refer to as "stakeholders" - customers, suppliers, shareholders, citizen groups, government regulators and the vast array of people with whom we deal in the course of operating a business enterprise. It was a wonderful experience.

Although I worked in the for-profit world, prior to serving on a college faculty, I know from many friends that their experiences in the non-profit world were just as satisfying.

I have noticed recently, though, that members of organizations seem to be exhibiting a somewhat lower awareness of the basic principles of personal behavior that we discussed earlier in this book, and which you will now have developed during your college career.

I am certainly not suggesting that people in organizations today are not well intentioned. But for some reason there appears to be a lower level of demonstrated business courtesy.

Why has this trend developed?

The world today has become increasingly more cost competitive on a global basis, with enormous emphasis on short-term profits and return on investment. Training programs in American organizations, reflecting this increased competition and complexity, often stress more the "what" than the "how to" of enterprise activity. Today, these programs concentrate primarily on the technical features and benefits of the organization's products and services, the competition, the marketplace dynamics, etc.

The sales training I once received addressed all of the above, but also included instruction on how to handle myself on the telephone and in written communications, how to conduct myself with customers, how to deal effectively in various social situations, and so forth.

Finally, and perhaps most importantly, the drive for immediate success in society has altered the way in which we view relationships in the professional world. Long-term relationships have given way to meeting short-term budgets and goals as the highest priority. Often, achieving short-term objectives comes at the expense of professional courtesy and its importance in building long-term relationships with business partners.

The good news for you, as a new graduate, is that you can build upon many of the personal skills you have been developing in college, and apply them to the workplace. I know for a fact that individuals with a well-developed pattern of personal behaviors stand an excellent opportunity in today's world to differentiate themselves from their competition. I'm sure that each of us prefers to do business with people we like, and attention to the practice of business courtesies is not only the right thing to do, it is also the profitable thing to do.

In this part of our book, then, I wish to focus your attention on two very important things.

The *first* is to continue to develop the personal skill set that you have begun to build in college, and which now needs to be adapted to the organizational setting. Proper and outstanding personal behavior will distinguish you from your peers, enhance your career opportunities for promotion and increased responsibility, and of course represent the "right" way to live.

It may take some time, but eventually it will be evident to you that you are always "on display" in an organizational setting, and impressions you make can be quite lasting. During my years in business, I certainly did not know all of our thousands of employees, but I would interact with many of them on an occasional basis. Maybe we were brought together at a managers meeting, or as part of a task force working on one project or another. Often, I would encounter employees from different operating groups, or from different functions, and my exposure to them would be relatively brief.

But I watched, and listened. I tuned in to comments people made, how they interacted with others, and in general how they presented themselves. The names of those who impressed me went on a list of names I kept in my desk drawer - and when I had openings to fill in my department, that list of names was the first thing I considered.

As an example, during a two-day meeting among many different employees to address issues regarding development of an effective workforce, I was particularly impressed with a woman who held a technical role in the company — but who exhibited an extraordinary ability to listen and understand other points of view. Her name went on my list, and when I had an opening for a Human Resource manager in my department, she got the job — and several future promotions in that function.

Your personal skill set can set you apart just as it did for this woman. It will be important for you to exhibit these skills every day. You will never know when someone is watching.

Secondly, while working as diligently as you can each day, you will also need to develop a "model" for your career. Just as you successfully thought through the choice of a major and a career while you were in college, now you need to think though the kinds of organizational experience and contributions you can make on the way to a satisfying and realistic culmination to your career. Remember the "win-win" language you used during your first job interview? Now comes the time to begin to put that theory into practice.

The following several chapters will focus on the personal skill set that will help you succeed in your daily work life. Chapter 14 will then discuss how to create your initial career model, and how to refine it over time.

CHAPTER 7

Effective telephone communications

I 'll always remember the phone call I placed in 1964 to Mr. Irenee DuPont, then Executive Vice President of the DuPont Company. I was a high school sophomore, and my classmate Joe and I had been given an assignment to interview someone of note in our community. Since we lived in Wilmington, DE, Mr. DuPont was an ideal choice.

I tried calling him at work, but couldn't seem to find my way through the maze of departments and switchboards. So I looked up his home number (it was listed) and called him that evening. I explained my situation, and he couldn't have been nicer on the phone. He asked when we wanted to come in for the interview, and agreed to Washington's Birthday - not because it fit his schedule, but because it fit our school vacation schedule. He gave us a full hour of his time that day, when he certainly had more pressing matters to deal with. I still have a copy of the interview, and I'll always remember his graciousness towards two high school kids.

I've thought of Mr. DuPont many times over the ensuing years, and I can think of no better example of how we can all conduct ourselves in a business setting. With that in mind, let's think about some basic behaviors that help to ensure success.

Basic telephone courtesies.

It amazes me how often people will use their voice mail to screen calls. I have no idea why that is, but it is - all too often. I recall the day I rode up on the elevator with a colleague. I exited the car on the 23rd floor, and she rode on up to the 24th floor, where her office was located.

As I entered my office, I remembered that I had a topic to discuss with her, and gave her a call, since I knew she was in her office. It went to voice mail, so I walked up the nearby steps — to find her in her office, reading a newspaper while her calls went to voice mail (and the phone had Caller ID). There I was, my name on her phone screen and now standing in her doorway, not 2 minutes later. I did not get a good impression of her at that moment, to say the least, and I still remember that incident when I think of her.

Somewhat the opposite experience occurred when my phone rang one time. I answered it, and the caller remarked. "Oh, you answer your own phone!" Um, sure, why wouldn't I? Business is business, so take things as they come, and have the courtesy to deal with callers on a real time basis, rather than engaging in tedious phone tag and/or voice mail exchanges.

This would be an excellent time to comment on voice mail, which can be very useful, if used properly.

Keep your voice email greeting up to date. You may choose to just have one generic greeting ("I'm sorry I am not available to take your call, please leave a message and I'll return your call as soon as possible"), and never change that greeting. Others will update their greetings on a daily basis, indicating if they are in the office, traveling, on vacation, etc., and leaving appropriate instructions to the caller. That's fine, as long as you remember to update the greeting! Often I have called an individual on, say December 15, only to encounter a greeting that he or she is "on vacation until November 30th, and will get back to you upon my return". This just sends your caller a message that you don't give a lot of attention to detail.

Avoid using internal voice mail as your primary means of internal company communication. I once worked for a great boss, but he communicated with all of us almost exclusively over voice mail. He may ask a question of seven of us, and then send each of our replies to the other six. It mushroomed out of control, and all of us spent hours listening to voice mails, responding, forwarding, and listening again. Much better, in my opinion, to use voice mail for the kinds of minor issues that can be handled that way, and use live direct or conference calls for the more serious matters. It is amazing how more efficient - and effective - that can be.

Always try to have a "landline" available for your use, especially on conference calls. I know that cell phones are quickly supplanting the land lines, but anybody who has participated in conference calls - and you will do so many times - can tell you that nothing beats a landline for clear, crisp communications. You may use your cell phone on individual calls, but conference calls demand better clarity that many cell phones can deliver. This is important, and I will return to this point a bit later.

Returning the call.

I know the dilemma. You've been in a 3-hour meeting, and have returned to your office to find numerous telephone message slips on your desk, plus another ten voicemails stacked up in your system. You're running behind on your schedule and therefore place the slips next to your phone, thinking you'll get to those calls and the voice mails later.

Later comes, perhaps the next day, or even several days later - or not at all. Meanwhile, the party has called again. Now you're too embarrassed to return the call - so you delegate it to someone on your staff. Not only have you not returned the original call promptly, you never returned it at all, and you've managed to create ill will in the process.

Often, opportunities between companies start with an unanticipated phone call. A caller may have read something about your firm, or heard something about you in particular, that has prompted a thought about a business opportunity that might be explored. All business partners met for the first time in some way. So, when someone calls you on the phone -- return the call! Perhaps you will find that the caller is better directed to another person in your organization. In that case, feel free to redirect the inquiry. But at least show people basic courtesy, and return the call. Others will appreciate it when you do - and remember if you don't.

My rule of thumb is that every call should be returned on the same business day, if at all possible. When you cannot do so because of prior commitments, hand the stack of messages to your assistant and ask the assistant to phone the callers to tell them that you're aware they called, that you are unavoidably committed for the rest of the day, and that you'll return the call first thing in the morning. In the meantime, if there's something that won't wait, perhaps the matter can be directed to someone else. At least such callers know that you value them and their relationship to you, and they are high on your priority list.

If you don't have access to an assistant, return the calls after business hours if necessary, before you go home. Leave messages on their voicemails, explain why you were unable to return the calls that day and tell them that you will try to reach them at the next opportunity.

Sometimes I will call a business associate's office, only to be told that person is traveling and won't be back in the office for several days, as if that somehow is a reason I cannot expect a prompt return call.

Business travel does not alleviate the responsibility of returning phone calls, although travel across international time zones does make this a bit more challenging. In this age of cell phones, voice mails, e-mails, texts and other forms of instant global communication, messages received in your office can be conveyed to you on a daily basis. Make a list of people you need to call, keep it in your pocket and use the inevitable waiting time (airports, train stations, etc.) to return the calls as soon as possible. Let's face it - we return the calls we want to return, so let's return all of them.

Calling a business colleague at home.

Since many people now list their home and/or mobile numbers on their business cards, and the pace of business today often requires people to reach each other at home after office hours, it's important to be sensitive to the needs of the person you are calling. Place yourself in your colleague's time zone, and ask yourself if you would be receptive to a call at that hour.

I once worked closely with a sales manager who lived on the West Coast, while I lived in the Philadelphia area. He was in the habit of calling me at home, almost daily, to address some issue that had arisen during the afternoon (his time). The calls always came at about 6:30 - 7:00 PM, when we were sitting down to dinner. Finally, I told him that I would be happy to talk to him from home on any evening at all - but to call me after 9:00 PM Eastern Time, after my then-young children had gone to bed and I had more time to talk. This, of course, meant that he had to call me after 6:00 PM in his time zone, during his evening hours at home. It was amazing how those many important issues could suddenly wait until the next morning, or be anticipated and dealt with during our overlapping businesses hours earlier in the day.

Advice for cell phone use.

Over the last two decades, we have seen nothing short of explosive growth in the cellular phone market. Particularly in the business community, cell phones are quickly becoming the primary means of contacting business colleagues who are working away from their offices, or even reaching them while they are in their offices, increasingly through the use of text messages as well as voice calls.

With this pervasive use of cell phones, it's probably a good idea to think about some common rules of business courtesy in these situations.

Most importantly, if you are in a meeting or attending a presentation in which others are involved, turn the phone off or place it in vibration mode. Allow your cell phone's voice mail or text system to take the message, with your voice mail greeting promising that you will check for messages frequently, and return the call promptly. Most phones can also be set to an auto-respond mode for incoming text messages as well.

If there is a pressing need to be interrupted during a meeting by an expected call, explain in advance to the other meeting participants that you may be interrupted for a call, and ask for their indulgence in this unusual situation. When the call comes, step outside the room to speak privately with your caller.

This applies to one-on-one meetings as well. Unless the call is expected and important, and you notify your colleague in advance, let the phone vibrate in your pocket. Continue to focus on your colleague, and get to the voice mail later.

Finally, try to be professional and select a ring tone that reflects a serious business approach. Loud, showy ring tones are unfortunately all too common, but they are unprofessional, show bad taste and should not be used in a professional environment.

CHAPTER 8

Effective written communications

Does anyone know where I can buy a stamp?

L etters, documents, emails, and text messages — all are in widespread use in business today, and all should be clearly and professionally written for the communication method being used. But let's start by discussing the most effective (and possibly most underused) form of written communication possible - the personal handwritten note.

I still consider the handwritten note one of the best ways to let others know that you appreciate doing business with them. It only takes a few minutes to write, but it has an impact far beyond the time invested. My recommendation is to use the personal note, and to use it often.

Although most employees don't have it, I think it's a plus to have a set of personalized notepaper. It can be your own personal stationary with your home address, or it can be a form of your organization's stationary, personalized for your use. You may wish to explore whether this might make sense for you, depending on the number of outside stakeholders with whom you come into contact as part of your responsibilities.

To mark the conclusion of a successful contract negotiation, as a thank-you for having enjoyed time spent together in a business context, or for myriad other business reasons, a personal note is always appropriate and appreciated.

These notes can also be used effectively to offer congratulations to a business associate on a promotion, to offer best wishes on a move to a new position or company, or to note some significant personal event, such as a recent marriage, the birth of a child, breaking 80 on the golf course (that would work for me!), etc.

Think about how often you receive a regular letter in the mail, handwritten and personalized for you — with a stamp! It's often the first thing that you open, and it can have the same positive impact for you with your business associates. Use it often, and well.

Business letters and memos.

You will write many of these, of course, during your career. Unlike texts and emails, which are generally used for brief messages and information sharing, these forms of written communications are used to address larger matters — such as describing the status of complex negotiations with a business partner, or recommending new products for launch. The list of topics is fairly endless, and it is these longer forms of written communication that demand organization, clarity and precision.

The fact that memos are longer than emails does not mean that they have to be extremely long. Challenge yourself to capture information in as succinct a way as possible. Your readers will appreciate it.

When you author internal memos and external letters, remember that your readership will ultimately be quite a bit larger than what you anticipated. These more significant communications often are shared more broadly in the organizations, and live on as future references. The good news is that a well-written document will help to showcase your understanding of the issues, as well as your ability to communicate effectively.

Therefore, take your time with these. Start with an outline, arrange the memo logically and use headings to help guide the reader through the document.

Begin with a concise statement of the issue, and end with a strong recommendation for further action, always inviting comments and suggestions from your readers.

CHAPTER 9

Proper behavior in meetings

No matter what type of organization you select for your career, one of the great rewards is the opportunity to meet a diverse group of people. All of them will have some impact on the work you do and your ultimate success, and many of them will become personal friends. You will want to develop a pattern of behavior that allows you to make the most of this rich experience.

I'm sorry, what was your name again?

Nothing is worse than forgetting the name of someone you just met, whether it is at an individual meeting or as part of a group discussion. It shows them that your attention is elsewhere, and that you do not value them as highly as perhaps you should. Since I have been guilty of this more than once, I'll offer some of the tools I developed to attempt to prevent this from happening.

When someone greets you, try to block out all other thoughts and focus on that person's name. Really focus on it, and try to relate the name to something you know well. For example, "Steve" might have the same name as your brother, or "Kristin" as your daughter. That will help.

Secondly, ask for the person's business card and keep it visible, especially in meetings. There is nothing wrong with arraying several cards on the conference table in front of you, arranged in the order in which people are seated.

I've found it an excellent way to keep the names straight, and as an aid in memorizing them.

To underscore how important this is, allow me to share a very embarrassing episode. I once flew from Philadelphia to San Francisco, where I met with our western region sales manager. Together, we went to the downtown office of a major potential customer to deliver a contract proposal. Our sales manager introduced me to the customer, and the three of us spent several hours discussing the many aspects of the proposal. By agreement, we then met for dinner that evening — and it quickly became obvious that the customer had completely forgotten my name. In conversation, my sales manager tried his best, saying things like "As Vic mentioned this afternoon....", but nothing stuck. I remained utterly nameless for the rest of the evening.

Now, this gentleman was a potential customer, so I had to let this affront pass. But if the shoe had been on the other foot, if I had been the customer and he had been making a proposal to me, what impression would I have received, and how likely would I want to deal with him further? Something to keep in mind.

Leave "side bar" conversations to the lawyers!

You've seen plenty of courtroom dramas on television. Often a judge will ask the lawyers for the plaintiff and the defendant to "approach the bench" to discuss a procedural matter out of earshot of the jurors. This is known in legal jargon as a "side bar" discussion.

These side bar discussions are fine in the courtroom, but not in the meeting room. Effective meetings demand the attention and participation of all the participants. If you have something to offer, offer it to everyone. If it is a somewhat off-topic point, jot it down and save it until the end of the meeting, when the organizer will usually ask if there is "anything else" for discussion. Do not, under any circumstances, begin to discuss your idea with the person next to you, while the meeting is going on. That is a "side bar" discussion, which is unwelcome in that situation and exhibits extremely rude behavior.

Power down those electronic devices.... and other suggestions.

It's important, so worth mentioning this a second time. Always mute your phone, laptop, tablet or Apple Watch (the list gets longer every year) when you are in a meeting. No one wants to hear ring tones blasting away while attempting to accomplish important work. A phone set on vibrate can be discreetly checked — but only if you are expecting an important call that you absolutely, positively have to take at that time. In these situations, please announce to your fellow attendees that you are expecting a call that is time sensitive, apologize in advance for having to answer it — and then do so outside the meeting room.

In large organizations, it is common for many of the employees to speak more than one language. Almost all meetings in the United States are conducted in English, so it is rude (and a bit unsettling) to have two people begin to converse in a language that others present do not understand. I've also seen this type of behavior at business dinners and other, less formal situations, and there is probably no faster way to earn mistrust from your colleagues.

You will be asked to participate in conference calls on a frequent basis, as companies use this as a substitute for more expensive business travel. It should go without saying that, for in-person meetings as well as conference calls, you should always be on time. If the conference call was scheduled for 10:00 AM, I always made it a point to dial in to the call center by 9:58. Your time is no more valuable than anyone else's, and it is important to always respect that.

There is one other point we covered earlier under proper telephone communications, but it is also worth repeating here. When on a conference call, remember to try to use a landline instead of a cell phone connection. It may not always be possible, but it increases the audio clarity for all who are on the call. In fact, if you work from a home office, I would urge you to have a land-line installed for all of the business calls you make and receive at that location.

If you need to present slides or video at the meeting, get the audio/visual equipment set up in advance, test it and make sure it is operating properly. There's nothing worse than people having to waste time while the presenter tries to get the projector to work.

A note regarding the one-to-one meetings.

Most sales and purchasing people will tell you that many of their meetings are not large affairs, but are simple one-on-one sessions where issues of a routine nature are discussed. Generally, these meetings occur in the office of one of the participants. A few suggestions relative to these small meetings are worth mentioning.

First, please do not answer your phone while meeting with someone in your office. This common incivility can offend even the most agreeable person. If you value the person with whom you are meeting, show your visitor the simple courtesy of giving your undivided attention. It's unfortunate that many of us violate this most basic of courtesies.

Second, be prepared for your visitor. Finish other business, have your assistant or voice mail system take incoming calls, and straighten up your desk area. This lets your visitor know that you have been expecting him or her, and that you value the time and effort your guest has made to see you.

CHAPTER 10

Organizing and leading the meeting

A s your career progresses, you will graduate from being a meeting attendee to assuming the roles of a meeting organizer and leader. This places an added responsibility on you to make sure that the meeting is planned effectively. At the same time, it offers you the opportunity to demonstrate good leadership and organization skills.

There is no doubt that a well-planned meeting, incorporating the proper participants, can be a very efficient way of pooling resources to reach a common objective. However, meetings that are not well planned or are poorly run can often lead to wasted time and effort all around.

At the outset, the organizer should clearly define the objectives and agenda for the meeting. Circulate these to the participants well in advance, and all those invited should be encouraged to offer their comments.

The organizer should then issue a final agenda, including the starting and ending times for the meeting. People have other matters to handle, and this will allow them to schedule their time appropriately.

Arrive at the meeting location early, and make sure that the room is set up with the right number of chairs, possible refreshments, A/V equipment in good working order, and to be sure that the room has not been double booked (a common occurrence). You may have an assistant that looks after much of this, but you are the meeting leader and need to ensure ahead of time that all is in order.

It often happens that out-of-town visitors will arrive well in advance of a meeting. The organizer should anticipate this, and be prepared to make visitors comfortable until the meeting starts. Some coffee, the Wall Street Journal, Wi-Fi access and the use of a spare office, are thoughtful ways to let your visitors know that you appreciate their attendance. At all costs, don't leave them sitting in the reception area. You invited them, so be prepared to host them.

One more note. In addition to being on time for meetings, greet the other participants, be polite and thank everyone for coming. It's amazing how many executives think they live beyond these basic courtesies.

In larger meetings, at which many of the participants are unknown to each other, it is important for the organizer to be prepared to formally introduce each attendee. This introduction should consist of each person's name, company affiliation, job title and the reason why each was invited to the meeting. The participants can then see that the organizer has put time and thought into the selection of the attendees, and it is infinitely preferable to the "everybody take a minute to introduce themselves" format which is most often used.

The organizer should conduct the meeting crisply, following the agenda that everyone has received, keeping to the agreed-upon finishing time, and summarizing afterward the action steps that have been identified. Most importantly, thank the participants for their willingness to attend, and offer to return the favor at a later date. All involved will leave knowing that they have been appreciated for their service.

CHAPTER 11

Negotiations

M any books have been written on successful negotiation strategy, but this is not one of them. As you can imagine, though, your personal approach and your degree of courtesy are extremely important in any negotiation, and often the difference between success and failure of the parties to reach agreement. *Remember, people do business with people they like.*

In my career, I have seen relationships damaged in the process of negotiation. Conversely, I have seen negotiations that were unsuccessful from a business viewpoint, but the participants remained on good terms and looked forward to the next opportunity when they might be able to do business together.

Setting the tone.

It is very important that a positive tone for the negotiations be established from the outset. Each party needs to be given the opportunity to set forth their expectations and needs, and to clearly define the objectives as they see them. During this initial phase, it is imperative that all participants listen attentively to gain a true understanding of the other party's objectives, hopes and concerns.

Following this, it is important for both parties to agree upon a mutual objective, which would yield a win-win outcome. At this point I would suggest that all of the objectives be reduced to writing, so that there is always an initial memorandum of understanding to fall back upon when the going gets tough, and all are in danger of temporarily losing their direction.

It is important to start with the big picture, and then work from there. Plunging prematurely into detail can often have the effect of derailing the negotiations quickly.

I am reminded of my first meeting with the executives of one of the nation's largest railroads. I had just taken over the position of General Manager for my company's distribution function, and my predecessor (who was retiring) accompanied me to an introductory meeting at the railroad's home office.

During the plane trip out, I showed my colleague the agenda I had prepared for the meeting. It began with a brief overview of our corporation, focusing on the outlook for all of our businesses. It then proceeded to update the railroad executives on the impact of some organizational changes, followed by some notes on my own background and philosophy of business. Only then did the agenda begin to list the key areas of opportunity between our two companies, and to set forth some possible joint agreements that might be considered.

My colleague was horrified at my approach. In his opinion, the railroad executives would have no interest in any of this preamble, and his view was that we ought to get in there and start banging on some existing contentious issues right away. "That's all they understand", he said.

I persuaded him to try things my way, and the railroad executives seemed pleased with my approach - an approach that allowed us to do many innovative things together over the ensuing years, to great mutual advantage. I learned from this experience that placing issues into a larger context was often a way to achieve desired results.

Where and when should we meet?

In terms of negotiation logistics, I always urge the parties to adopt a "home and home" approach to the negotiations, so that each side has an equal opportunity to avoid the hassles and cost of travel. If one party (usually the customer) insists that all meetings are held on their home turf, the customer is unconsciously erecting barriers to success.

The party hosting a particular negotiation session should go out of its way to accommodate their visitors — suggestions for hotels, hotel reservations themselves, perhaps have a car meet them at the airport, or schedule a break in the meetings to take them to a point of local interest. Show them that you value them as business partners, and are willing to do the small things that always make such a positive impact.

Follow up each negotiating session with a letter, summarizing the progress to date and the key action steps for the next meeting. This will not only ensure that all pre-work is properly completed, but it will help to avoid misunderstandings. Perhaps the party who did not have to travel for that particular session could volunteer to write the letter. The tone of the letter should be positive and recap the outcome of the last session, identifying the path forward and the next steps that were agreed upon by the participants.

Handling the inevitable disagreements.

In any negotiation, there will inevitably be times of serious disagreement over certain issues. The key here is to keep the disagreements confined to the business at hand, and not let them become personal differences.

I'd suggest that these sensitive matters always be handled in person - not by letter, and certainly not by voice mail. Serious hitches in negotiations must be handled carefully and courteously.

On the occasion of a particularly difficult negotiating session, I would suggest the meeting be preceded by a small dinner, with only the key participants in attendance. The dinner should be hosted by the local party, or the party whose turn it is to act as host. There should be an agreement up front that this dinner is only for the purpose of a careful airing and explanation of the key troublesome issues. Keep it focused, and keep it polite. Select a quiet restaurant, where you will not be rushed.

The idea is to hold off on the detailed negotiations until the following morning, and to allow each side to talk about major concerns over dinner. Then, each of the parties can reflect on the conversation overnight, and frequently the parties will develop creative solutions to offer in the next day's negotiating session.

In my experience, this approach will go a long way toward keeping the negotiations moving forward, and maintaining cordial relationships. I know that the "expense account meal" is under attack, but I have found it - when judiciously used - to be an important factor in business success.

How can we wrap up the successful - as well as unsuccessful - negotiation?

When the negotiations are finally over, and a resolution is reached, by all means take the time and consideration to mark the event appropriately. As mentioned in the last chapter, small but thoughtful mementos are a fine way of letting people know that you appreciated the time and effort that went into the negotiating process, and that you value them as individuals.

To mark the successful outcome, try to be creative and offer a memento that will have ongoing relevance to the new business arrangement. In one case, after we negotiated an unusual 10-year agreement with a new supplier, we gave all of the key participants (on both sides) a small rosewood box that contained a clock — and an inscription marking the duration of the agreement.

When the negotiation does not yield a successful outcome, a letter to the other party is appropriate — expressing disappointment that things did not work out, stating that you understand the reason, and expressing a desire to work together in some other way in the future. Just because the "deal" didn't materialize does not mean that you don't want to work with the same people again.

CHAPTER 12

Can we get personal, one more time?

W e discussed the topic of personal deportment earlier in the book. While it is important to develop the proper personal style on campus, it is even more important in the workplace — where your career advancement is at stake.

Nothing tells us more about individuals than the way they carry themselves - how they behave toward others and how they react to people around them, particularly in difficult situations.

Although a person's individual actions combine to form one composite (favorable or unfavorable) impression, there are certain elements of behavior that can be examined individually. When each element is given the attention it deserves, an overall favorable image emerges.

Let's spend a few moments, and discuss some of the most important aspects of proper deportment in the organizational environment.

It all starts with proper language.

You know the word. It begins with an "F".

It's not a nice word, but we hear it all the time. Along with other similarly offensive words, I have found it used all too commonly in the professional world, as the general quality of discourse in America has been "defined down".

More than anything else, the increasing use of bad language in general has been a barometer of the decrease in business courtesy over the last 15 years.

It's been pervasive, with slang and off-color jokes creeping into the vocabulary of senior and junior professional people, male and female alike. Why? Perhaps its part of the effort to be "macho" and to let one's colleagues and competitors know how tough a person is.

The end result, though, is just a bad impression. The use of offensive language and off-color jokes only results in demeaning the people with whom you are speaking. It lets them know in a subtle way that you don't hold them in enough regard to keep the conversation on an appropriate level.

It's natural to get emotional from time to time, and to vent frustration. But this can be done in measured terms, and the impact of the message will not be lost. The message is likely to be enhanced when you choose your words carefully and with restraint. To use off-color language forces the listener to focus on the language itself, instead of on your message.

So please don't use bad language. Number one, you may not know how serious a negative impact it may have on the listener, who might be more sensitive to such language than you think. But more importantly, its use indicates that you are willing to stoop to a lower level in your choice of vocabulary. This can have no other practical effect than to tarnish your image as a professional person.

Akin to the choice of language is the tone and volume that you employ. Guard against using any tone that appears condescending or pompous, as it is an immediate turn-off to your audience. Similarly, the office environment is simply no place for raised voices, either on the phone or in personal conversations. Shouting only indicates that you have lost control of a situation, and is extremely disruptive to those around you.

Everyone deserves respect.....everyone.

Every organization is arranged in a type of hierarchy, with the management team at the top and the rank and file employees organized into various reporting relationships.

Simply put, we should show respect for the dignity of all employees and colleagues, regardless of their positions in the organization. The same deference shown to the CEO should be shown to administrative assistants, mailroom clerks, telephone operators, receptionists, etc.

Take the time to learn the first names of as many people as possible throughout your organization. Ask occasionally about their families and other aspects of their lives that are important to them. Send a short sympathy note to those who have had deaths in the family, or a get-well card to someone who is having a serious bout with illness. The recipient will remember these simple acts of respect and kindness, and will be more committed to you and the organization as a whole.

I recall an occasion in which we were celebrating the successful startup of a new manufacturing operation. A dinner was held near the facility, and many employees from the local facility were invited. A group of us flew out in the company plane from our home office, and during the flight I asked our two pilots to join us for the celebration dinner. As I was introducing various individuals during the dinner, I made sure to introduce the pilots, along with the other guests who were attending the event.

The manufacturing plant in question was by far our largest, and the pilots had flown there literally hundreds of times. To my surprise, I discovered later that this was the first time anyone had asked them to participate in a company event, even though they were just as much company employees as we were.

Not too long afterward, I was a guest at a football game, in a box owned by another firm with whom we did business. The chairman of the firm was present, graciously greeting and spending time with each of the twenty or so guests who had been invited. Sitting toward the rear of the box were three gentlemen who introduced themselves to me as the host's driver and the two company pilots - very much enjoying the football game while they were on a trip away from home. Clearly, their CEO took a personal interest in them.

Your office organization says something about your personal organization.

Always try to maintain a neat, organized office or work space. Visually, it gives people a good idea as to whether you are an orderly, methodical business-person - or whether you're the type of person who probably forgets appointments, is slow to return phone calls, etc.

Look around you and you'll see both kinds of offices. First, there's the orderly office environment in which everything appears to have its place and priority. Then there's the office space that looks like a tornado hit it, with everything thrown into various piles.

With which person would you rather do business? While fully admitting that I am a "neat-nick", to me the answer is obvious. So be sure to maintain a good, organized environment for your colleagues and your visitors. It shows respect for them, and gives an indication of the orderly manner in which you handle your own responsibilities.

In the same vein, make sure that your personal appearance matches that of your professional looking office. Dress neatly and appropriately, don't slouch or put your feet on the desk, and always rise to greet visitors.

OK, so what does "dressing appropriately" really mean?

Many organizations today have chosen to allow casual attire on certain days, or every day. Although I know many people who believe that the traditional business suit (and tie for men) is the preferred manner of dress, it's clear that casual dress is probably here to stay in many organizations.

It's unfortunate that, once "business casual" dress codes were put into place, many companies later had to clarify what constitutes acceptable casual business attire. They had to prohibit the type of clothes you might wear to a ballgame, or to work around the house. I simply urge everyone to dress appropriately for business, at all times.

The way we dress often says volumes about the degree of importance with which we regard our business associates. We dress tastefully and neatly for many personal social occasions, and the same should hold true for the office environment. Bear in mind, too, that you can never be sure what circumstances will occur during the course of the day, and what places you may unexpectedly be required to go before the day is out. You certainly want to be dressed appropriately for any reasonable eventuality, and need to keep this in mind. Dress for what *might* happen today, not what you *think* will happen.

My personal experience, which I offer for your consideration: I have on occasion felt underdressed, but never have I felt overdressed.

Dealing with personal conflict in the workplace.

It is inevitable that well-intentioned people will occasionally disagree with one another over business matters, and sometimes the disagreements can run deep. Often, there will be an urge on the part of one person to vent frustration to a colleague. This should be done, but handled properly, as it often helps to get things out into the open.

Be sure to handle this sensitive discussion on a personal basis, one to one. Do not under any circumstances use voice mail, e-mail or text as a vehicle for communicating your frustration. That will simply result in a return volley from behind the electronic protective shield, and make it more difficult for both parties to meet and settle their differences. When you have a serious disagreement with another person, use the phone or, better yet, a personal meeting to discuss the issue openly and honestly. You'll be amazed at how well things can sort themselves out in short order.

Everyone in a supervisory position must deliver constructive criticism from time to time. Unfortunately, we can probably all recite cases where the criticism was delivered publicly, and in a non-constructive fashion.

Professional deportment requires that performance discussions be carried out in private, very objectively and courteously. It should always be prefaced with the statement that the criticism will be constructive, and is meant to improve job performance. It is not meant as a reflection on the employee's character, but as a periodic job training aid.

Finally, remember the golden rule, and always treat others as you would like to be treated in a similar situation.

CHAPTER 13

Making the most of social events.

A requirement of most professional positions today is attendance at the occasional social function, whether as part of a large group (such as those which occur at conventions) or as part of a smaller function, at which only a few people are involved.

I know many individuals who would personally rather not attend these events, but the nature of business today is such that occasional attendance really is appropriate to maintaining good business relationships. Once again, however, we must keep in mind that proper courtesy is expected in this area also, and there are some things that should be kept in mind.

Responding to the invitation.

Invitations to these events arrive in many ways - by formal note, e-mail, telephone call, direct personal contact, etc. The favor of a prompt response is always appreciated. Often, organizations are left in a quandary as to how many people to expect at a social function, due to the slowness of response by some invited guests. Usually, this leads to a follow-up phone call to the invitee, asking whether or not he or she plans to attend. By all means, try to respond promptly - within a week, I would say, is the ideal.

Some people think that if they do not plan to attend, then no response is necessary. On the contrary, it is always appropriate to acknowledge an invitation, either way. A short note back to the sender is the best response, thanking your host for the thoughtfulness, and giving a good reason why you cannot attend the function. By putting yourself in your host's shoes, you will understand why the reply and prompt acknowledgment is always appreciated.

Should your spouse or a guest also be invited, by all means discuss the invitation between yourselves before you respond, and then commit for one or both of you, as the case may be. It is amazing to me how many times I have seen individuals accept an invitation, and then back out at the last minute because they suddenly realized that there is a conflict with the spouse's schedule. Some prior communication here goes a long way.

Finally, be sure to show up! If there is one practice I would be tempted to rank at the top of the list of discourteous behavior, it would be the thoughtlessness of people to accept an invitation and then simply not show up. It happens all too often, is an affront to your hosts, and ends up costing them a good deal of unneeded expense.

Sometimes you may wish to include an additional person as part of your party when attending a social event. This usually can be handled gracefully, but it is important to check with your host beforehand. Explain why you would like to bring an added guest, and ask if that would pose a problem. This is a basic courtesy that should be extended to your host. Please don't simply arrive, uninvited guest in tow.

Now, make the most of the occasion.

One memorable evening, during the course of a convention, my wife and I were asked to join a business associate and his wife for dinner. Also invited were several other couples, and we formed a circular table of ten people. Coincidentally, both couples on either side of us were extremely quiet during the entire meal. Try as we might, we could not get more than a simple "yes" or "no" from them during the entire evening. After a tremendous amount of effort, we simply gave up, listened politely to the conversation on the other side of the table, spoke with each other, and ended the evening at the first opportunity.

Fortunately, this experience is the exception rather than the rule. Usually, we find our business colleagues to be witty, articulate and interesting people. However, I know that these situations can and do happen during these types of social affairs, so try your best to be as engaging as possible.

The message here is to make the most of the social function. Take the opportunity to get to know your business colleagues and their spouses or guests. Ask about their backgrounds - where they were born and grew up, how they met and how they came to their present position. Ask about their interests, their families, and their future plans. Remember that everyone likes to be asked about themselves. As I mentioned previously, people do business with those whom they like.

The situations just described apply generally to those occasions in which you and others are together in a small group for some extended period of time, perhaps over dinner, at a sporting event, etc. Often, however, you will find yourself at a large reception, involving hundreds of people. For these situations, in-depth discussions are not usually possible or appropriate, but there are certain other rules of the road that can be kept in mind.

Be sure to mingle, and let others do the same. The purpose of these functions is usually to provide an opportunity for a large number of people to say hello and to meet one another. This is best accomplished if you gradually walk through the room, greeting people as you encounter them. Usually just a few minutes of conversation is appropriate - introductions, job responsibilities and geographical location are usually enough. After a discussion along these lines, exchange business cards and find a polite way to end the conversation, such as "Well, I'll look forward to seeing you during the course of the meeting". Then break away politely in order to make your next introduction.

By all means don't ensconce yourself by the bar or the buffet table, or stand in a corner, waiting for the world to beat a path to your door. Work the room, and make the effort to initiate conversations. For people who tend to be on the shy side, I know how difficult this can be. However, it will become easier with practice, and you will find the evening to be much more interesting and fulfilling.

Speaking of ensconcing yourself by the bar, always keep in mind that these functions are about business, and you should never let alcohol in any way interfere with your ability to act in a completely professional manner.

CHAPTER 14

Creating your career model

During the early stages of my career, I was quite focused on what my next promotion might be, and what I should be doing to get to that next level. Then, somewhere along the line, I started focusing instead on my current job and performing it as well as I could. The result was remarkable; the more I applied myself to the task at hand, the more my career moved in an upward direction.

This is not to say, though, that you should not spend at least some time thinking about the long arc of your career. It's important to have a vision of what you think you can accomplish, in what type of organization that might occur, and to generally formulate a plan that may allow you to realize your full potential.

Up to this point, my book has focused on advice that can help you better perform the "task at hand" — the day-to-day dealings in your professional life. Attention to the details we have been discussing will help you "polish" yourself, and will place you in line for career advancement.

Bear in mind that organizations are primarily concerned with the interests of the organization. Your interests usually come second. But this does not necessarily have to be the case, and your own careful career planning can demonstrate that your personal advancement can complement the organization's need to develop competent managers.

There are many good books published on the subject of career management, but allow me to share some thoughts that might apply during the early years of your career.

First, think about what type of position you would like to have as a capstone for your career. It might be in the area of finance, marketing, non-profit services administration, high level individual contribution, etc. The possibilities are almost endless. But, just as you did when you started thinking about career options in college, think broadly and then refine the list to the possibilities that you think make the most sense and which may be the most achievable.

Next, try to seek out people that currently hold these positions, and ask them what types of work they did along the way. What types of positions taught them the most in terms of useable skills? How did they apply that knowledge in later positions? Don't be shy. Remember the story about Mr. DuPont. Most people will only be too willing to share information with you.

Once you have an idea of the end point, and the intermediate steps that might lie along the way, draw up your own career "straw model". As the term implies, it is likely to change — and should, as you move through your career and fine-tune your objectives. Discuss this model with management and human resources every few years. Identify for them the positions that might make sense for your next step— in terms of what you can bring to the position, and what the new position will teach you for the one after that. Basically, you are creating a "win-win" career plan — one that is good for the organization, while also satisfying your own personal goals.

When a position opens up in the organization that matches one of the "way stations" you have identified in your straw model, discuss with management how this might be a logical next step in your longer term plan. You will be surprised to see how well your candidacy is accepted.

CHAPTER 15

My wish for you

I would like to thank you for taking the time to read and reflect on the contents of this small book. In thinking about what to include, I purposely avoided diving too deeply into any one subject. There are plenty of books out there that deal extensively with one or more of the topics upon which we have touched.

My goal was two-fold. First, to draw attention to specific behaviors that I always found present in successful students and employees. Second, to more clearly link the college and workplace experiences — four years on campus goes by in the blink of an eye, and these years are an important time to build a foundation for what comes next.

Always remember that you are surrounded by people willing to help in any way they can - parents, teachers, counselors, friends, fellow students and professional colleagues. Do your best to treat them with thoughtfulness, respect and courtesy. Work hard. Enjoy life. The journey is marvelous.